MACHINES ★ AT WORK

TRACTORS

BY HAL ROGERS

THE CHILD'S WORLD® • MANKATO, MINNESOTA

The Child's World®

Published in the United States of America by The Child's World®
1980 Lookout Drive • Mankato, MN 56003-1705
800-599-READ • www.childsworld.com

PHOTO CREDITS
© Charles O'Rear/Corbis: 7 (main)
© iStockphoto.com/Bjorn Heller: 3
© iStockphoto.com/Cathleen Abers-Kimball: 20
© iStockphoto.com/Diane Diederich: 12
© iStockphoto.com/Guillermo Perales Gonzalez: 19
© iStockphoto.com/Jason Lugo: 8
© iStockphoto.com/Jerry McElroy: 4
© iStockphoto.com/Mike Clarke: 7 (inset)
© istockphoto.com/Robert Pernell: 15
© iStockphoto.com/Roman Milert: cover, 2
© iStockphoto.com/Sreedhar Yedlapati: 16
© Les Greenwood/Alamy: 11

ACKNOWLEDGMENTS
The Child's World®: Mary Berendes, Publishing Director;
Katherine Stevenson, Editor

The Design Lab: Design and Page Production

LIBRARY OF CONGRESS CATALOGING-IN-PUBLICATION DATA
Rogers, Hal, 1966–
    Tractors / by Hal Rogers.
        p. cm. — (Machines at work)
    Includes bibliographical references and index.
    ISBN 978-1-59296-959-3 (library bound: alk. paper)
    1. Farm tractors–Juvenile literature. I. Title. II. Series.
    S711.R57 2007
    629.225'2–dc22   2007013406

 **Contents**

This huge tractor is used on a farm in Nebraska.

 ## What are tractors?

Tractors are powerful **vehicles**. They might not move fast. But they are built to do hard work. They can pull or push very heavy loads. Many tractors are used on farms. But tractors do other jobs, too!

5

What parts do tractors have?

The driver uses **controls** to run the tractor. On many tractors, the driver sits in a **cab**. Tractors sometimes tip over. The cab keeps the driver safe. Other tractors have an outside seat. A seat belt and roll bar keep the driver safe.

The main photo shows a tractor with a cab.
The small photo shows a tractor with a roll bar.

Here you can see some of the engine parts on an older tractor.

 Tractors do heavy work. They need a big **engine** to provide power. The engine's power moves the tractor. It can run other tools and machines, too.

What are tractors used for?

Different kinds of tractors do different jobs. Farm tractors often pull other machines. They pull **plows** to get fields ready for planting. They pull machines that plant seeds or pick crops. They do other farm work, too.

10

This farm tractor is getting a field ready for planting.

This man is mowing the grass in his yard.
The big black box holds the grass clippings.

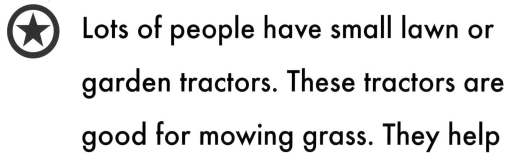 Lots of people have small lawn or garden tractors. These tractors are good for mowing grass. They help with other yard work, too.

13

Sometimes tractors have a big **blade** on the front. The blade can easily push dirt, rocks, or snow. Bulldozers are tractors with blades. Bulldozers also have **crawler tracks** instead of wheels. Crawler tracks move well on bumpy ground or soft dirt.

Some bulldozers have flat blades. Others have blades that are curved.

crawler tracks

blade

bucket

This loader's deep bucket can hold lots of dirt.

 Loaders are tractors with a bucket on the front. The bucket picks things up. Loaders work in all kinds of places. They move rock and dirt. They move trash at city dumps. They even move snow.

Diggers are tractors with a **backhoe**. The backhoe has a long arm. The arm has a bucket on the end. The backhoe digs and scoops dirt and rocks.

18

backhoe

bucket

⭐ This digger's backhoe is being used to scoop sand.

This tractor is being used to plow a field of rye.

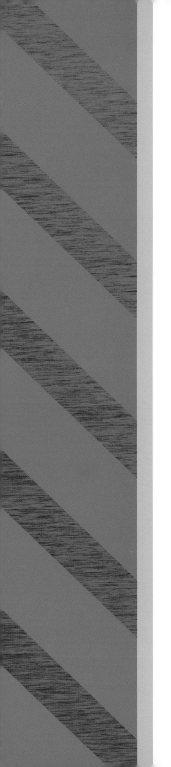

Are tractors important?

Tractors are used all over the world. They pull heavy machines. They plow fields. They push dirt and snow. They dig holes. They help people build things. Tractors are very important!

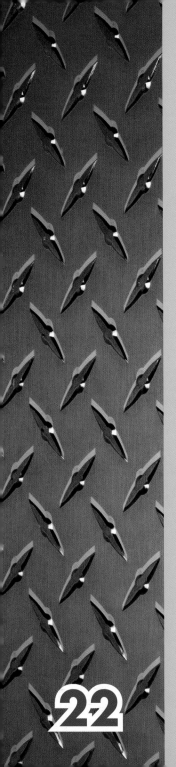

 # Glossary

backhoe (BAK-hoh) A backhoe is a digging scoop on a long arm.

blade (BLAYD) A blade is a part that is broad, flat, and usually thin. The blade on a tractor pushes things.

cab (KAB) A machine's cab is the area where the driver sits.

controls (kun-TROLZ) Controls are parts that people use to run a machine.

crawler tracks (KRAWL-er TRAX) Crawler tracks are metal belts that some machines use for moving.

engine (EN-jun) An engine is a machine that makes something move.

plows (PLOWZ) Plows are tools that turn soil and break it up before it is planted.

vehicles (VEE-uh-kullz) Vehicles are things for carrying people or goods.

⭐ Books

Bingham, Caroline. *Tractor.* New York: DK Publishing, 2004.

Nelson, Kristin L. *Farm Tractors.* Minneapolis, MN: Lerner Publications, 2003.

Ransom, Candice F., and Laura J. Bryant (illustrator). *Tractor Day.* New York: Walker & Company, 2007.

Young, Caroline, Steve Page, Teri Gower (illustrator), and Chris Lyon (illustrator). *Tractors.* London: Usborne Publishing, 2003.

⭐ Web Sites

Visit our Web page for lots of links about tractors:
http://www.childsworld.com/links

Note to parents, teachers, and librarians: We routinely check our Web links to make sure they're safe, active sites—so encourage your readers to check them out!

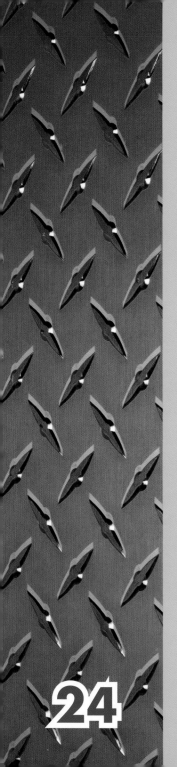

 # Index

 # About the Author

Hal Rogers has written over a dozen books on machines and trucks. A longtime resident of Colorado, Hal currently lives in Denver, along with his family, a fuzzy cat named Simon, and a lovable dog named Sebastian.